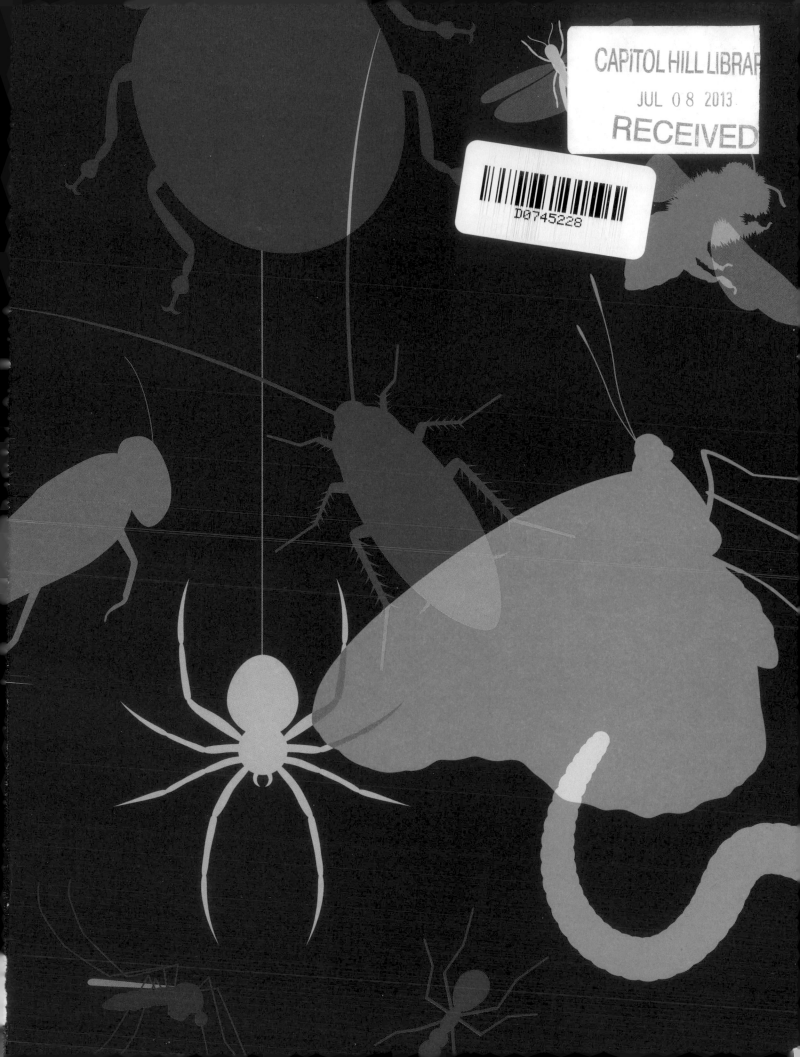

In the same series by PatrickGeorge:

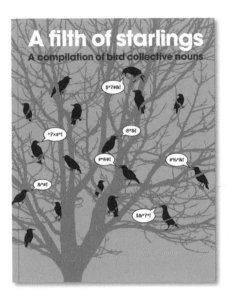

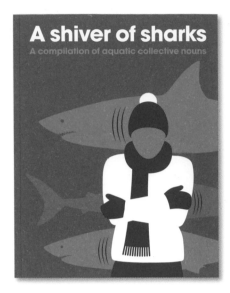

© PatrickGeorge 2012

Illustrated, designed and published by
PatrickGeorge
46 Vale Square
Ramsgate
Kent CT11 9DA
United Kingdom

www.patrickgeorge.biz

ISBN 978-1-908473-00-4

British Library Cataloguing in Publication Data.
A catalogue record for this book is available from the British Library.

Printed in China.

A crackle of crickets

A compilation of insect collective nouns

PatrickGeorge

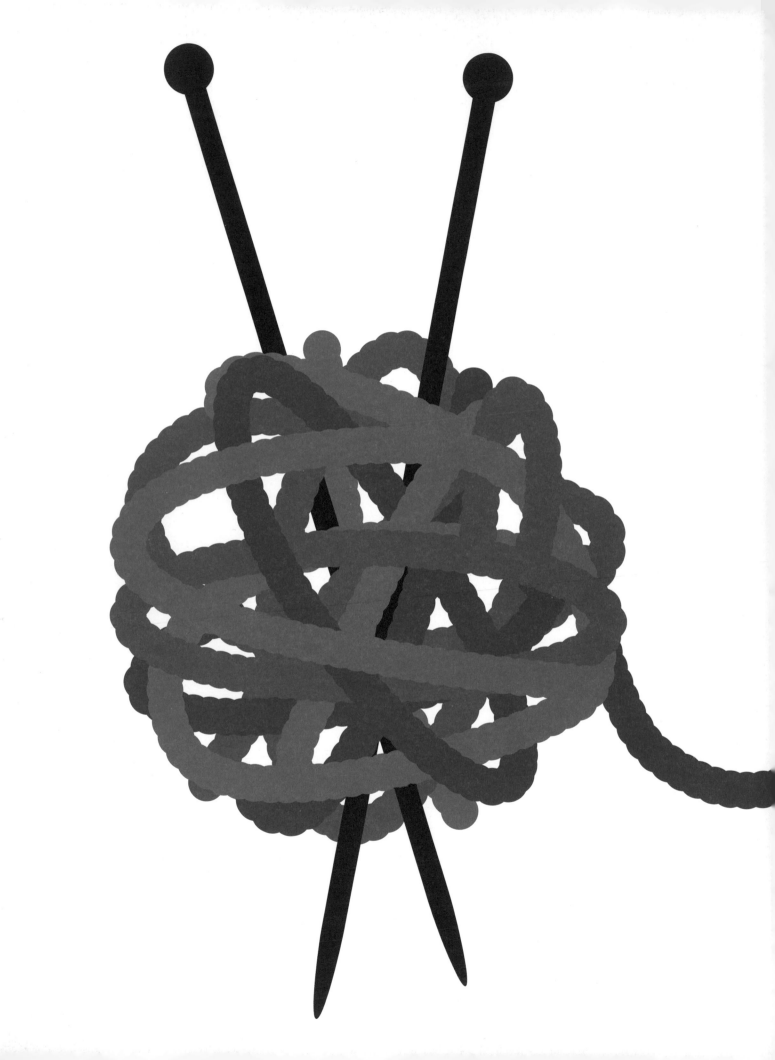

A clew of worms

Whether it's a ball of wiggling worms in your compost, a fat worm burrowing through the soil or being plucked by a blackbird, the earthworm is a welcome sight. For a creature with no arms, legs or eyes, it is pretty amazing – a natural waste disposal unit, chewing, grinding and processing organic matter to enrich our earth.

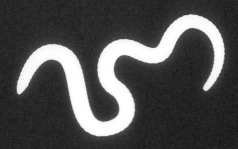

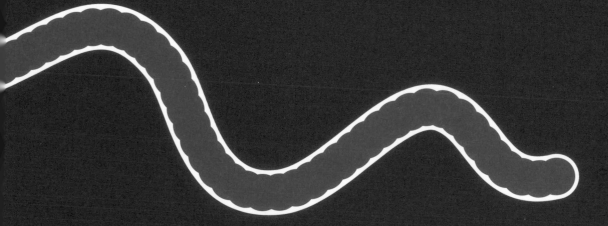

A loveliness of ladybirds
Like the beautiful butterfly, the lovely ladybird
is actually telling its predators how disgusting
it tastes. It secretes an unpleasant substance
to protect itself and its bright colour and spots
serve as a reminder to others to stay away.

A venom of spiders

The black widow spider will inject venom into its prey to paralyze or kill it. You'd be unlucky if it were you but you probably wouldn't come to as much harm. The most unlucky, and unlikely, victim is the black widow's partner who she is known to kill after mating, hence her name.

A conflagration of fireflies

Some fireflies flash to attract a mate, some flash to lure their prey, and some flash to warn their predators of their unpleasant taste. In certain parts of the world, thousands congregate in the evenings to flash in unison, creating a wonderful and spectacular conflagration, glittering and sparkling in the night sky.

A culture of bacteria
Bacteria and Art – culture that can be grown or culture that we grow to appreciate. Bacteria come in a wide range of shapes and forms and can be found in every habitat on Earth from acidic hot springs to animal matter. Apparently, there are approximately ten times as many bacterial cells as human cells in the human body alone!

A ghost of gnats
Appearing as a ghostly swarm at dusk, gnats hover
silently in the air getting into your hair and under
your clothing, unnoticed and barely visible, causing
you to itch and scratch. They will haunt your kitchen
bins and hatch out as quickly as you eradicate
them – a presence you could do without.

A bike of hornets

Larger and louder than a wasp and with a reputation of being aggressive, the hornet is actually a docile creature and will only use its powerful sting if threatened. Protective of their nests, they will attack if disturbed and then it would best to get on your bike and be on your way!

An army of caterpillars
Marching and munching its way through the leaves,
this eating machine prefers to remain unseen, often
working under cover of night, hiding underneath the
leaves so that its cover isn't blown. Some species of young
caterpillar also build a web in which they live, to defend
themselves, before dispersing when nearly fully grown.

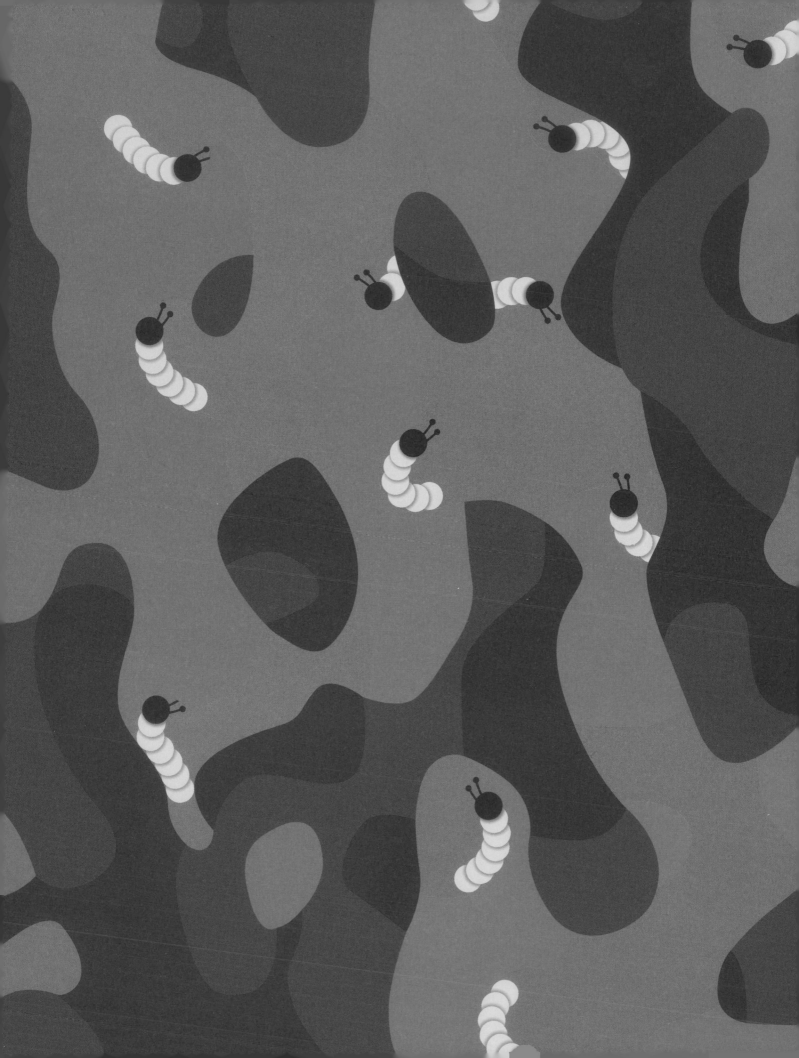

A flock of lice

Lice will flock in human hair and combing them out of young children's hair is a chore. Much as we hate them though, they've been around for ages and are probably here to stay, with evidence suggesting they might have existed as long ago as the age of dinosaurs.

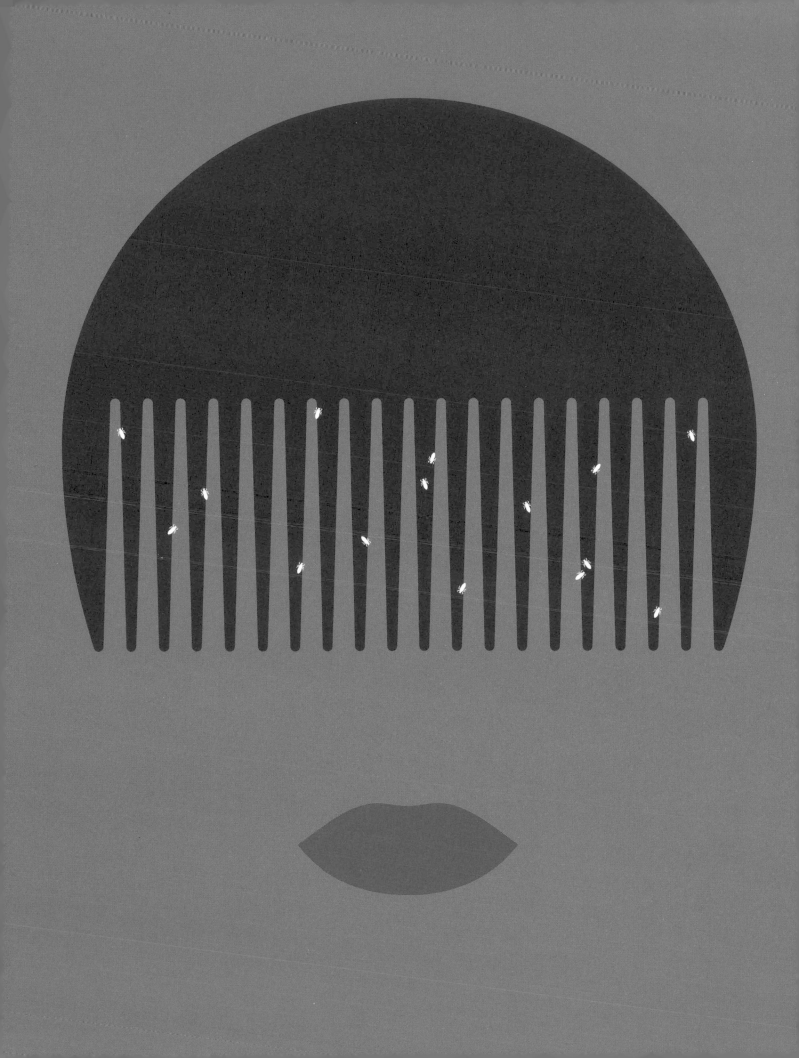

A crackle of crickets

It's a hot, sultry night and the crickets are chirping –
a crackling, background noise on a summer's evening.
Did you know that as the temperature rises, the
cricket's song becomes louder and faster? Apparently
you can work out the temperature pretty accurately
too – just count the number of chirps in 14 seconds
and add 40 to get the temperature in Fahrenheit.

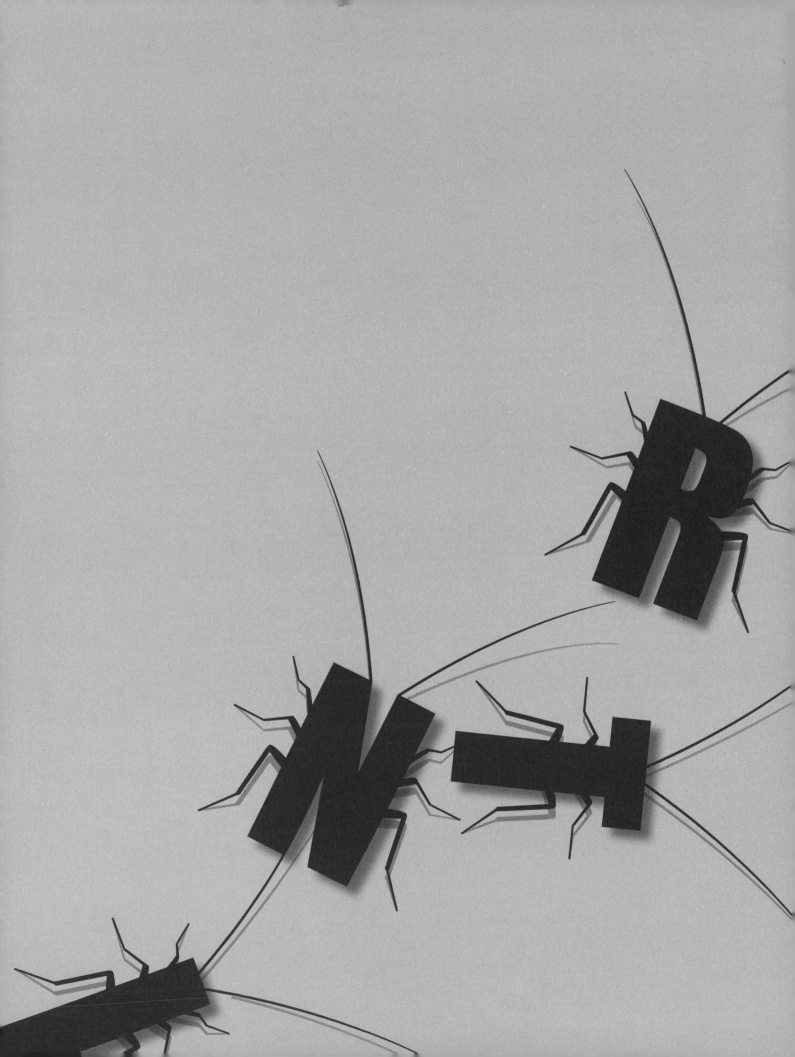

An intrusion of cockroaches

Unwanted, these intruders aren't easy to get rid of. Known for being able to survive extreme conditions, cockroaches can go without food or water for up to a month, surviving on very limited supplies, and can go without air for up to 45 minutes, slowing their heart rate right down. Admirable qualities maybe but these creatures are commonly known to disgust.

A kaleidoscope of butterflies

With its kaleidoscopic wings, constantly shifting and changing, the fragile and vibrantly-coloured butterfly uses its myriad patterns to good effect. This dainty, beautiful creature warns predators with its colours that it is foul-tasting and poisonous. Birds stay well away!

A scourge of mosquitos

The mosquito is a scourge of our society: a pain and an itch you shouldn't scratch. They feed on nectar but the female mosquito also needs the iron and protein from our blood to produce eggs and will fly for miles at night to get its fill.

A hive of bees
The queen bee stays in the hive, laying eggs for a new generation. Her hive of worker bees will visit up to 500 flowers before returning home. And if she dies, another bee will be chosen and fed with royal jelly to make it fertile – and so life goes on.

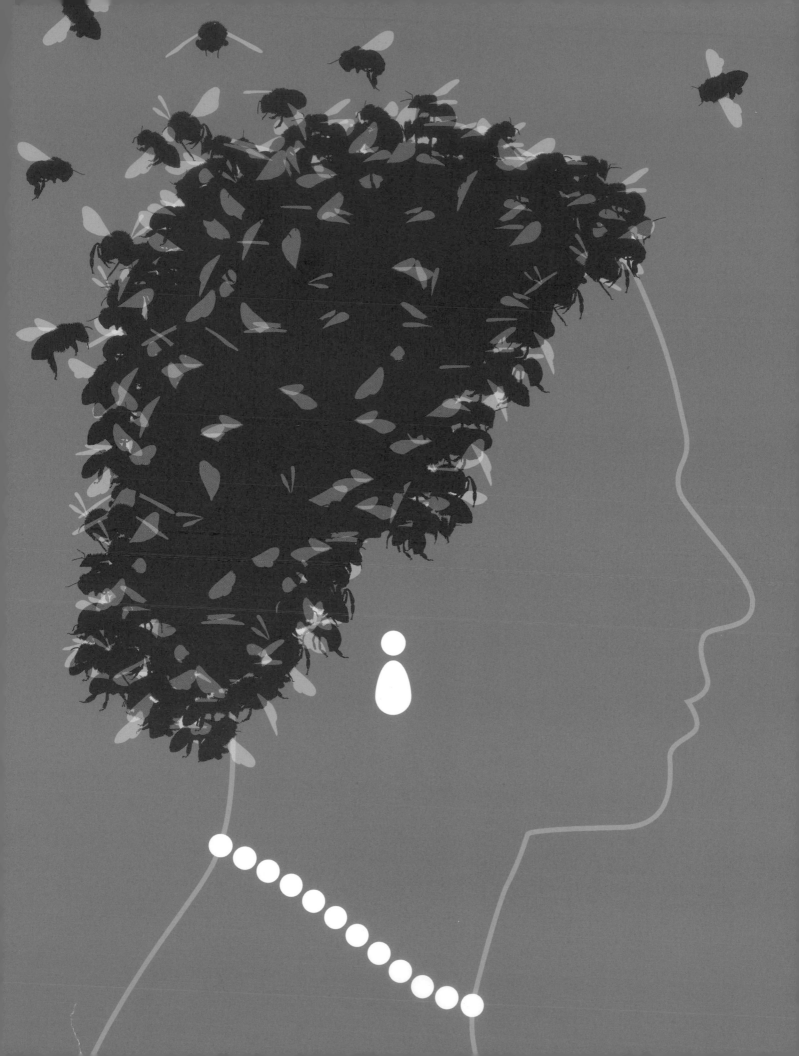

A cloud of grasshoppers

Did you know that the grasshopper is considered a good source of protein, vitamins and minerals in some parts of the world and can be cooked in many different ways? To escape predators however, they catapult into the sky, sometimes jumping 20 times the length of their own body. If they take off in a swarm, they are often referred to as a cloud.

A pail of wasps

Wasps don't wish to be a nuisance but they can't resist the bright colours, smells and sugary foods of a late summer picnic. So if they are really getting in the way, hang a ripe piece of fruit over a bucket of water and wait for the wasp to devour it. Full up, it will fall into the water below…

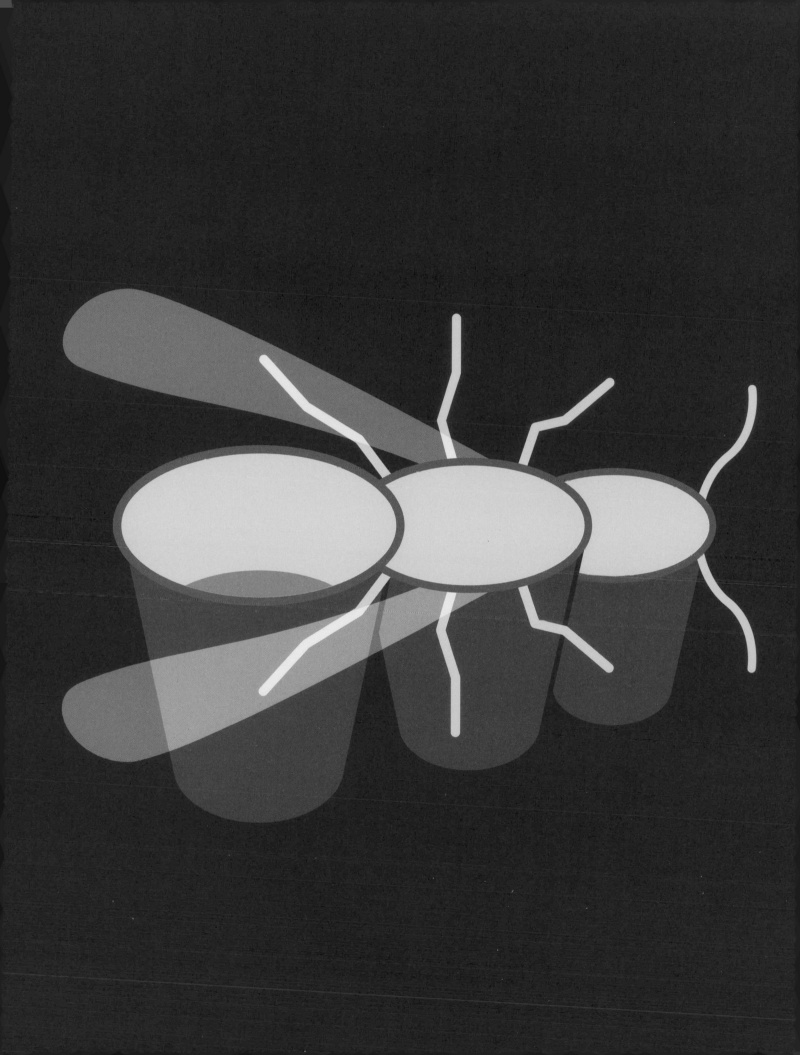

A plague of locusts

As rapid, widespread and deadly as a plague, locusts travel in swarms, stripping plants, trees and crops leaving nothing behind. Helped by the wind, they spread, infest and infect, causing harm. And once food sources run low, it seems that they turn upon each other. From death, there is no escape.

A colony of ants

Leaf cutter ants, bullet ants, trap-jaw ants… the list is endless.
Trap-jaw ants propel themselves into the air using their jaws
to escape predators. Doing it *en masse* they create an effect
of exploding popcorn. They also use their jaws to snap at
their prey 2,300 times faster than the blink of an eye.

A hatch of fleas

One flea can lay more than 20 eggs a day, some of which will hatch within two days. Multiply that by ten, twenty, thirty fleas and you can see how quickly they can infest your home. They can also jump incredibly fast and far, about 200 times as high as their own body.

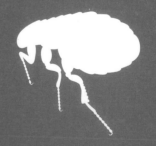

A business of flies

Flies are often perceived as dirty and as a nuisance but we all appreciate how useful they are. They're always busy – and we need their business, whether it's clearing up rotting matter or being used as bait. Maggots found on dead bodies can help forensic scientists determine how long a body has been dead.